Hard Cover Trade Edition
Atlantic Canada Distribution By
Nimbus Publishing Limited
P.O. Box 9301, Station A
Halifax, Nova Scotia
B3K 5N5

Soft Cover Edition
Distribution By
H.H. Marshall Ltd.
3731 MacIntosh Street
Halifax, Nova Scotia B3K 5N5

Edited by Anna Hobbs
Artwork preparation by
Ambrose, Koo & Associates, Toronto
Printed in Hong Kong by
Everbest Printing Co. Ltd.

All book photographs available from
Master File, Stock Photo Library
415 Yonge Street, Suite 200,
Toronto, Canada M5B 2E7

Cameras: Pentax 6x7
and Contax with Carl Zeiss T. Lens
Films: Fujichrome, and Kodachrome

ISBN: 0-9690520-4-9

Planked Salmon recipe on page 49 courtesy Bowater Mersey Paper Company
Vegetable Chowder recipe on page 43 courtesy Nova Scotia Department of Agriculture
Baked Scallops recipe on page 27 courtesy by Nova Scotia Department of Fisheries
Recipes on pages 20, 28, 38, 40, 54, 59,from a collection of Hines family favorites
All remaining recipes supplied by the Nova Scotia Department of Agriculture
and are re-printed by permission of Canadian Living Magazine.

NOVA SCOTIA PICTORIAL COOKBOOK

Photographs by Sherman Hines
Edited by Anna Hobbs

Westhouse Publishing
2319 Brunswick St.
Halifax, N.S.
B3K 2Y9

Introduction

Eating well has been a way of life in Nova Scotia since 1606 when the French explorer Samuel de Champlain established North America's first gourmet club, l'Ordre de Bon Temps (The Order of Good Cheer) at the tiny settlement of Port Royal. Created to raise the spirits of the 15-man company throughout the long winter months, each man took his turn as host of the day to produce a sumptuous feast.

From the time of this first settlement, situated across the river from present-day Annapolis Royal, the history of Nova Scotia has been closely linked with the foods that a fertile land and bountiful sea have provided. Each region within the province has its own way of preparing and enjoying nature's goodness. The dishes now considered Nova Scotia specialties have developed as settlers from different countries adapted local products to their own recipes. The Scots who loved good baking brought oatcakes and Bannock. The United Empire Loyalists who emigrated from the United States brought baked beans. The Germans who settled in the Lunenburg area of the South Shore liked spicy and pickled foods, such as marinated herring or Solomon Gundy.

Ever since the 1860's when the railroads and steamships began to bring visitors from Upper Canada and the eastern U.S.A., Nova Scotia has been charming tourists with its love of good food, its warm hospitality and its beautiful scenery.

Enjoy here a sampling of its best tastes and spectacular vistas.

ld Stone House, Poplar Grove   The Habitation at Port Royal

Blue Rocks

Dublin Shore

BROILED OR BARBECUED SWORDFISH STEAKS

Swordfish is a dinner favorite in Nova Scotia. A versatile local catch, it's delicious broiled in the oven or on the barbecue.

2 lb	swordfish steaks, 1/2 to 3/4 inch (1 to 2 cm) thick (fresh or thawed)	1 kg

Marinade:

1/4 cup	soy sauce	50 mL
1/4 cup	orange juice	50 mL
2 tbsp	ketchup	25 mL
1 tbsp	lemon juice	15 mL
1	clove garlic, chopped	1
2 tbsp	chopped parsley	25 mL
1/2 tsp	oregano	2 mL
1/2 tsp	pepper	2 mL

Clean steaks and place in shallow pan. Combine marinade ingredients. Pour over steaks and marinate 2 hours in refrigerator. Place steaks on greased broiler pan. Baste with marinade and cook 4 to 5 inches (10 to 12 cm) from heat for 8 minutes. Turn, baste and cook 5 minutes longer or until fish is firm and flakes easily with fork. Or, cook fish in same manner on greased grill on barbecue. Makes 6 servings.

Peggy's Cove

Cape Forch

BRAS D'OR TROUT
WITH MUSHROOM SAUCE

This special breed of rainbow trout is reared in the salty water of the Bras d'Or Lakes.

2	rainbow trout (each 12 oz/340 g)	2
3 tbsp	butter	50 mL
1/2 lb	mushrooms, sliced	250 g
1	clove garlic, chopped	1
	Salt	
	Freshly ground pepper	
2 tbsp	light cream	25 mL
1 tbsp	butter	15 mL
1 tbsp	all-purpose flour	15 mL
1/2 cup	light cream	125 mL
	Chopped fresh parsley	

Clean fish and pat dry with paper towels. In skillet, melt 3 tbsp (50 mL) butter; sauté mushrooms until tender. Add garlic, salt and pepper to taste and 2 tbsp (25 mL) cream; simmer gently 2 to 3 minutes.

Arrange trout in buttered baking dish. Cover and bake in 375°F (190°C) oven until fish flakes easily with fork, 15 to 20 minutes.

In saucepan, melt 1 tbsp (15 mL) butter; whisk in flour. Add remaining cream and whisk until smooth and thickened. Remove cooked trout from oven; drain liquid and stir into cream sauce. Pour sauce over fish. Garnish with parsley. Makes 2 servings.

Upper Great Brook

MAPLE BAKED BEANS

Here's a hearty bean dish with a maple flavor.

4 cups	white beans (Great Northern, navy or lima beans)	1 L
12 cups	cold water	3 L
5	slices bacon, cut in 1 inch (2.5 cm) pieces	5
1	onion, sliced	1
1 cup	maple syrup	250 mL
1/2 cup	chili sauce	125 mL
1 tsp	salt	5 mL
1 tsp	dry mustard	5 mL
	Boiling water	

Soak beans in cold water overnight. Drain and place half of beans in casserole; add bacon, onion and remaining beans. Combine half of maple syrup with chili sauce, salt and mustard; pour over beans. Add boiling water to cover and bake, covered, in 300°F (150°C) oven 4 hours. Add remaining maple syrup as liquid is needed. Makes 12 servings.

CARROT CAKE WITH MAPLE CREAM FROSTING

Here's a Nova Scotia variation of a well-known favorite.

1 cup	all-purpose flour	250 mL

1 tsp	baking powder	5 mL
1/2 tsp	baking soda	2 mL
1/2 tsp	salt	2 mL
1 tsp	cinnamon	5 mL
1/2 tsp	ground ginger	2 mL
1/2 tsp	ground cloves	2 mL
2/3 cup	cooking oil	175 mL
1 cup	granulated sugar	250 mL
2	eggs	2
1 cup	grated carrots	250 mL
1/3 cup	chopped walnuts or pecans	75 mL

Sift together flour, baking powder, soda, salt, cinnamon, ginger and cloves. In large bowl, beat together oil and sugar; beat in eggs, one at a time. Add dry ingredients; mix well. Fold in carrots and nuts.

Pour batter into greased 8-inch (20 cm) square cake pan. Bake in 350°F (180°C) oven 50 minutes or until tester inserted in centre comes out clean. Let cool 10 minutes; remove from pan and place on rack to cool. Frost with Maple Cream Frosting (recipe follows).

Maple Cream Frosting:

1	pkg (1/4 lb/125 g) cream cheese, softened	1
1 tbsp	maple syrup	15 mL
1-1/2 cups	icing sugar	375 mL

Beat together cream cheese and maple syrup until smooth. Gradually beat in icing sugar and beat until smooth.

CROCKPOT LAMB STEW

Poplar Grove

Crockpot stews are especially tasty when made with Nova Scotia lamb.

2 lb	boneless stewing lamb or 3 lb (1.5 kg) bone-in	1 kg
2 tbsp	oil	25 mL
1/3 cup	all-purpose flour	75 mL
2 tsp	salt	10 mL
1/8 tsp	pepper	1 mL
1	clove garlic, crushed	1
1/2 tsp	thyme	2 mL
4 cups	water	1 L
1	onion, sliced	1
6	medium carrots, diagonally cut in 1-inch (2.5 cm) pieces	6
6	potatoes, peeled and quartered	6

Trim and discard excess fat from meat and cut meat into 1-1/2 inch (4 cm) pieces. In skillet, brown meat in oil; sprinkle with flour and brown again lightly. Place in crockpot with remaining ingredients. Cook on medium setting until meat and vegetables are tender, 8 to 10 hours. Serve with Curried Dumplings (recipe follows) if desired. Makes 6 servings.

Curried Dumplings:

1 cup	sifted all-purpose flour	250 mL
2 tsp	baking powder	10 mL
1/2 tsp	salt	2 mL
1/2 tsp	curry powder	2 mL
2 tbsp	shortening	25 mL
1/2 cup	milk	125 mL

Sift together dry ingredients. Cut in shortening until mixture resembles coarse crumbs. Stir in milk to make soft dough. Drop by spoonfuls onto hot stew. Cover and cook 20 to 25 minutes without lifting lid. Makes 6 dumplings.

New Ross Road

Peggy's Cove

The Middle Deck Restaurant, Halifax

BOILED FRESH
NOVA SCOTIA LOBSTER

Lobsters are at their best when prepared as simply as possible a
served either hot or cold, shelled or in the shell, accompanied w
melted butter, lemon wedges or mayonnaise. For each pou
(500 g) of live lobster, you get about 1/4 pound (125 g) of cook
meat.

Fill a large deep saucepan or soup kettle with enough water
cover lobster(s) and add 1/4 cup (50 mL) salt for each 4 cups (1
water. Bring water to rapid boil. Plunge in lobster(s); cover a

return to gentle boil. Cook 15 minutes for 3/4 to 1 pound (375 to 500 g) lobsters; 20 minutes for 1 to 1-1/4 pound (500 to 625 g) lobsters.

Remove lobster(s) from water and cool quickly under cold running water; drain. Turn each lobster on its back, and with a sharp knife, carefully split lengthwise down the centre. Then crack the large claws.

If removing meat before serving, discard the dark vein running the length of the tail, the small sac at the back of the head and the spongy grey tissue on either side of the back. Separate, but do not discard, the bright green liver (called the tomalley) and the red roe (if present); both are delicious.

LOBSTER NEWBURG

While Nova Scotians generally enjoy lobster at informal gatherings, it's also a natural for formal entertaining. Here's a favorite version of Lobster Newburg.

1-1/2 cups	frozen lobster meat, thawed and drained (reserve liquid)	375 mL
1/2 cup	butter	125 mL
1/3 cup	all-purpose flour	75 mL
1/4 tsp	salt	1 mL
1 cup	milk	250 mL
2	egg yolks, beaten	2
2 tbsp	dry sherry	25 mL
	Hot rice, toast points or patty shells	

Measure liquid from drained lobster meat and add enough water to make 3/4 cup (175 mL). In large saucepan over medium heat, melt butter; whisk in flour and salt until mixture is smooth, about 1 minute. Combine reserved lobster liquid, milk and egg yolks; gradually add to flour mixture in saucepan, stirring constantly over medium heat until thickened.

Cut lobster meat into bite-sized pieces and add to saucepan; simmer until lobster is hot. Remove from heat; stir in sherry. Serve over hot rice or toast points or in patty shells. Makes 5 or 6 servings.

◄ Peggy's Cove

LOBSTER CHOWDER

1	medium sized onion, chopped	1
2 tbsp	butter	25 mL
2	medium sized potatoes, diced	2
1 cup	water	250 mL
2 cups	lobster meat, cut up	500 mL
1 tsp	salt	5 mL
1/4 tsp	pepper	1 mL
2 cups	milk	500 mL
1 cup	light cream	250 mL
1/4 cup	butter	50 mL

In deep saucepan, sauté onion in butter until tender. Add potatoes and water; cover and simmer 10 minutes or until potatoes are almost tender. Add remaining ingredients. Reheat; do not boil. Makes 4 servings.

Peggy's Cove

FRUIT COMPOTE

Here's a dessert that incorporates the best of a bountiful harvest.

1	pear, peeled, cored and cubed	1
1	peach, peeled, pitted and sliced	1
1	Cortland apple, peeled, cored and sliced	1
1/2 cup	cherries, pitted	125 mL
3	plums, halved and pitted	3
1 cup	sliced strawberries	250 mL
1/4 cup	granulated sugar	50 mL
1/2 cup	water	125 mL
	Yogurt (optional)	

Prepare fruit and put in serving dish; chill. In saucepan, combine sugar and water. Bring to boil; reduce heat and simmer 3 minutes, then chill. Pour cold syrup over fruit. Refrigerate to blend flavors. Serve topped with yogurt if desired. Makes 6 servings.

STRAWBERRY-RHUBARB DELIGHT

Prepare this tasty nutritious dessert ahead of time and let it chill overnight in the fridge.

Crust:

1-1/2 cups	graham-wafer crumbs	375 mL
1/2 cup	melted butter	125 mL
1/4 cup	granulated sugar	50 mL

Filling:

2	pkg (each 1 tbsp/15 mL) unflavoured gelatin	2
1 cup	granulated sugar	250 mL
1/4 tsp	salt	1 mL
2	eggs, separated	2
1 cup	milk	250 mL
1 tsp	each of lemon juice, grated lemon peel and vanilla	5 ml
3 cups	creamed cottage cheese	750 mL
1 cup	whipping cream	250 mL

Sauce:

2 cups	chopped rhubarb (fresh or frozen)	500 mL
1/2 cup	granulated sugar	125 mL
1/4 cup	water	50 mL
1 cup	sliced strawberries (fresh or frozen)	250 mL
2 tsp	cornstarch	10 mL
1 tbsp	cold water	15 mL

Crust: Combine ingredients and press over bottom of 10-inch (25 cm) springform pan. Bake in 350°F (180°C) oven for 10 minutes; let cool.

Filling: In saucepan, combine gelatin, 3/4 cup (175 mL) sugar and salt. Stir in egg yolks and milk; cook over low heat until gelatin dissolves. Stir in lemon juice, peel and vanilla. Refrigerate until mixture mounds slightly when dropped from spoon.

In blender or food processor, process cottage cheese until smooth; stir in gelatin mixture. Beat egg whites until frothy; gradually add remaining 1/4 cup (50 mL) sugar, beating until stiff and glossy. Whip cream until stiff peaks form. Fold egg whites, then whipped cream, into cottage cheese. Pour mixture into crust; refrigerate overnight.

Sauce: In saucepan, combine rhubarb, sugar and water; cook over low heat until rhubarb is tender. Add strawberries, then cornstarch dissolved in cold water. Cook, stirring until mixture is thickened. Let cool. To serve, cut dessert into wedges and top each slice with sauce. Makes 12 servings.

KERST KRANSJIS

These are a special Christmas favorite of the Dutch families living on the South Shore.

1-1/4 cups	butter	300 mL
1	egg, separated	1
	Granulated sugar	
3 cups	all-purpose flour	750 mL
	Ground or slivered almonds	

Beat butter until soft and light. Add egg yolk and 3/4 cup (175 mL) sugar; beat 2 minutes longer. Add flour, 1 cup (250 mL) at a time, beating well after each addition.

On lightly floured board, knead dough until smooth. Roll out to 1/4 inch (5 mm) thickness. Cut into rounds about 2 inches (5 cm) in diameter. Make small hole in centre (use thimble) for wreath effect.

Place on greased baking sheet. Brush each with egg white; sprinkle lightly with sugar and almonds. Baked in 325°F (160°C) oven for 10 to 12 minutes. Makes 60 cookies.

Blue Rocks

Peggy's Cove

LUNENBURG SAUSAGE

This spicy sausage dates back to the time when Lunenburg families visited one another in the fall to see who had the heftiest pigs.

10 lb	ground pork	5 kg
2 lb	ground beef	1 kg
1/2 cup	ground coriander	125 mL
1/2 cup	salt	125 mL
1/4 cup	pepper	50 mL
1/4 cup	allspice	50 mL
2 cups	warm water	500 mL
	Sausage casings (optional)	

Combine all ingredients except casings and mix well. Test for seasoning by frying a small amount of meat mixture; taste and adjust seasoning. Stuff sausage into casings or form into patties.

In large skillet, fry sausage (in batches) over medium heat for 15 to 20 minutes or until evenly browned on all sides. Freeze up to 3 months, if desired. Makes 12 pounds (6 kg).

Lunenburg

Stonehurst East.

BAKED SCALLOPS

1 lb	fresh scallops	500 g
1/2 cup	cracker crumbs	125 mL
1/2 cup	bread crumbs	125 mL
1/2 cup	butter, melted	125 mL
2/3 cup	milk	150 mL
	Salt and freshly ground pepper	

Rinse scallops; pat dry. In small bowl, combine cracker and bread crumbs and butter. Sprinkle layer of crumbs in bottom of greased 4-cup (1 L) shallow casserole. Cover with scallops. Pour half of the milk over. Season with salt and pepper to taste. Top with remaining crumbs. Pour remaining milk over crumbs. Bake in 375°F (190°C) oven until crumbs are browned, about 25 minutes. Makes 6 servings.

STEAMED MUSSELS

Two types of mussels are found along the Nova Scotia coastline — wild and cultivated. Wild mussels grow in dense clusters, attached to rocks, piers and submerged objects. Summer beach parties along the South Shore often feature wild mussels steamed over a bonfire. Cultivated mussels are commercially farmed in collectors, entirely free from the ocean floor which produces a cleaner, more meaty product. Here is a tried-and-true method for steaming cultivated mussels at home.

Scrub the shells until clean. (The beards on mussels are easier to remove after cooking.) Place mussels in large soup kettle with 1/2 to 1 inch (1 to 2.5 cm) water. Cover tightly and steam over medium heat until shells open, 5 to 8 minutes. Discard any shells that don't open. Serve immediately with bowls of broth (reserved cooking water combined with melted butter).

Digby Scallop Fleet

Mussels

SOLOMON GUNDY

6	whole salt herring	6
2	onions, sliced	2
2 cups	vinegar	500 mL
2 tbsp	pickling spice	25 mL
1/2 cup	sugar	125 mL

Remove heads and tails from herring. Clean inside and remove skins. Fillet each herring as follows: Lay fish on one side with tail toward you. Using knife with sharp flexible blade, cut along backbone, from head to tail, exposing backbone. Cut down to backbone behind gills to detach fillet from head. Holding head end of fillet, slice down length of fillet between flesh and ribs and remove. Some bones may remain attached to flesh; carefully remove with fingers or tweezers. Cut flesh away from skin. Repeat with second fillet.

Cut into pieces about 1 inch (2.5 cm) thick. Place in bowl and pour in cold water to cover; let stand overnight. Drain excess water from herring.

In large glass jars, alternately layer herring and onions. In saucepan combine vinegar, pickling spice and sugar; bring to boil stirring constantly. Remove from heat and let cool. Pour over herring and onions in jars, filling to within 1/2 inch (1 cm) of top.

Halifax Harbour

Herring Fishing, Cherry Hill

Berwick

SAUERKRAUT SALAD

This tangy salad can be stored in the fridge for up to two months.

2 lb	sauerkraut, drained	1 kg
1	green pepper, finely chopped	1
1	large onion, chopped	1
2 cups	finely chopped celery	500 mL
1 cup	grated carrot	250 mL
1/2 cup	white vinegar	125 mL
1 cup	granulated sugar	250 mL
1/2 cup	vegetable oil	125 mL

In large bowl, mix together all ingredients. Place a weighted plate on top for 1-1/2 hours to press out excess liquid; drain well.

Store in covered container(s) in refrigerator. Makes 10 cups (2.5 L).

Blue Rocks

SOUTH-SHORE BOILED DINNER

Boiled dinners like this one provided a hearty meal for fishermen.

1 lb	salt cod	500 g
1/2 lb	pork fat, diced	250 g
6	carrots, halved	6
1	small turnip, cut in pieces (optional)	1
4	potatoes, peeled	4
4	small onions	4
1 tbsp	butter	15 mL
1 tbsp	all-purpose flour	15 mL
1/2 tsp	salt	2 mL
1 cup	milk	250 mL
2 tbsp	chopped parsley	25 mL
2	hard-cooked eggs, sliced	2

Cover salt cod with cold water; soak overnight. Drain; cover with fresh water and bring to simmer. Drain; taste and repeat if cod is still too salty. Drain well and keep warm.

In skillet, fry pork fat until crisp (these are called scrunchions) and set aside. In boiling water, cook vegetables until tender.

Prepare white sauce: In small heavy saucepan over low heat, melt butter. Add flour and salt; stir together until smooth. Gradually stir in milk; cook, stirring constantly, until thickened and smooth.

Arrange salt cod on heated platter; arrange vegetables around fish. Pour white sauce over fish. Garnish with parsley, egg slices and scrunchions. Makes 4 servings.

Berwick

ANNAPOLIS VALLEY APPLE PIE

3/4 to 1 cup	granulated sugar	175 to 250 mL
1/4 tsp	apple-pie spice	1 mL
Pinch	salt	Pinch
6 cups	thinly sliced apples (peeled)	1.5 L
	Pastry for double-crust pie (9 in/23 cm)	
1 tbsp	butter	15 mL
1 tbsp	lemon juice	15 mL

Combine sugar (use lesser or greater amount depending on tartness of apples), apple-pie spice and salt. Arrange sliced apples in layers in pastry-lined pie plate, heaping in centre and sprinkling each layer with sugar mixture. Dot top with pieces of butter. Sprinkle lemon juice over all. Cover with top pastry; seal and flute edges. Cut slits in pastry to vent steam.

   Bake in 450°F (230°C) oven for 10 minutes, then reduce heat to 350°F (180°C) and bake 45 to 50 minutes or until apples are cooked. Makes 6 servings.

Stonehurst East

WIGWAM CROQUETTES

In the beginning were the Micmacs, the native Indians of Nova Scotia. This Indian dish made with fish from the Fundy is delicious served with a creamy white sauce.

2 lb	white fish	1 kg
2 cups	milk	500 mL
1/4 cup	butter	50 mL
2 tbsp	finely chopped onion	25 mL
1 tbsp	thyme	15 mL
2 tbsp	all-purpose flour	25 mL
2 tbsp	lemon juice	25 mL
1 tsp	cold water	5 mL
1	egg, beaten	1
	Salt	
	Freshly ground pepper	
	Breadcrumbs	

Boil fish until it flakes; drain and let cool. In saucepan, bring milk to boil; add butter. Combine onion, thyme, flour and lemon juice; stir into milk. Stir over medium-low heat until sauce is thickened. Add water and remove from heat. Stir in beaten egg.

Flake fish and season with salt and pepper to taste; add egg mixture. Form into wigwam shapes. Place in shallow baking dish and cover with breadcrumbs. Bake in 350°F (180°C) oven 30 minutes. Makes 4 to 6 servings.

BLUENOSE FISH CHOWDER

No one knows whether it was the Acadians or the New Englanders who invented chowders, but everyone agrees that Nova Scotians have perfected them.

1 lb	fish fillets (fresh or frozen)	500 g
1/4 lb	pork fat, diced, or 6 slices bacon, chopped	125 g
1/3 cup	chopped onion	75 mL
2 cups	diced potatoes (peeled)	500 mL
2 cups	water	500 mL
2 tsp	salt	10 mL
1/4 tsp	pepper	1 mL
2 cups	milk (at room temperature)	500 mL

Cut fresh fillets into 3 or 4 pieces or frozen ones into 1-inch (2.5 cm) squares. In deep saucepan, fry pork or bacon until crisp; remove from pan and use for garnish.

Drain all but 2 tbsp (25 mL) of fat from pan. In remaining fat, sauté onion until tender. Add potatoes, water and seasonings; cover and simmer 10 minutes, or until potatoes are almost tender. Add fish; cover and simmer until fish is cooked, 5 to 8 minutes. Gradually pour in milk. Reheat; do not boil. Garnish with fried pork or bacon. Makes 4 servings.

BREAST OF DUCK MARGAREE

1	duck	1
	Salt and freshly ground pepper	

Brown Duck Sauce:

1	duck carcass (reserved from recipe above), cut in pieces	1
1	carrot, coarsely chopped	1
1	onion, coarsely chopped	1
4	stalks celery, coarsely chopped	4
2 cups	water	500 mL
6	black peppercorns	6
1	bay leaf	1
	Salt	
2 tbsp	butter	25 mL
2 tbsp	flour	25 mL
1 tbsp	tomato paste	15 mL
2 tbsp	butter	25 mL
1	shallot, minced	1
	Half clove garlic, crushed	
1 tbsp	Grand Marnier liqueur	15 mL
1/4 cup	apricot juice	50 mL
12	green peppercorns	12
1	apricot, sliced	1

Remove breast from duck; reserve.

Brown Duck Sauce: In large pot, cook duck pieces, carrot, onion and celery in small amount of oil until browned. Add water, black peppercorns and bay leaf. Bring to boil; reduce heat and simmer for 1-1/2 hours. Remove fat and scum from surface of stock. Remove meat and bones, reserving for some other use. Strain and season with salt to taste.

In saucepan, melt 2 tbsp (25 mL) butter; blend in flour. Cook until flour is browned; do not allow to burn. Stir in tomato paste; blend. Gradually pour in stock, stirring constantly. Cook sauce over low heat for about 1 hour or until smooth and thickened. Taste and adjust·seasoning, if necessary.

Meanwhile, season duck breast with salt and pepper to taste. In small roasting pan, place breast skin side down. Roast in 400°F (200°C) oven for 15 to 20 minutes or until meat is still slightly pink.

In skillet, melt 2 tbsp (25 mL) butter. Add shallot and garlic and cook until tender. Add liqueur; ignite with long match. Douse flame with apricot juice. Cook until liquid is reduced by half. Stir in 1/4 cup (50 mL) of the sauce. Strain into separate saucepan; add green peppercorns. Stir in 1 tbsp (15 mL) butter to add sheen to sauce; keep warm over low heat.

To serve, thinly slice meat and arrange on platter. Pour sauce over. Garnish with apricot.

FLORENCE HINES'S OLD FASHIONED MINCEMEAT

2 cups	cooked ground venison	500 mL
3 cups	diced peeled tart apples	750 mL
1 cup	ground suet	250 mL
3/4 cup	seedless raisins	175 mL
3/4 cup	currants	175 mL
3/4 cup	venison stock	175 mL
1/2 cup	apple jelly	125 mL
1-1/2 cups	packed brown sugar	375 mL
1/2 cup	apple juice	125 mL
1 tsp	each ground cinnamon and cloves	5 mL
1/2 tsp	each grated nutmeg and allspice	2 mL
1/2 cup	brandy	125 mL

In large heavy saucepan, combine all ingredients except brandy. Bring to boil; reduce heat and simmer for 1 hour, stirring often. Remove from heat; let cool. Stir in brandy.

Using funnel, fill sterilized jars to within 1/4 inch (5 mm) of top. Wipe rims; seal and store in cool place.

Whitetail Buck

BARBECUED BEEF RIBS

The tangy marinade imparts a wonderful flavor to barbecued ribs.

3 lb	beef spareribs	1.5 kg

Marinade:

1 cup	ketchup	250 mL
1 cup	water	250 mL
1/4 cup	honey	50 mL
1/4 cup	Worcestershire sauce	50 mL
1/4 cup	vinegar	50 mL
1 tbsp	celery seeds	15 mL
1 tsp	chili powder	5 mL
1 tsp	salt	5 mL
1/8 tsp	freshly ground pepper	1 mL
Dash	Tabasco sauce	Dash

Marinade: In saucepan, combine ingredients. Slowly bring to boil, stirring occasionally; let cool. Pour marinade over ribs; cover and let marinate in refrigerator 8 to 10 hours. Drain, reserving marinade.

   Place ribs on grill 5 inches (12 cm) from hot coals. Cook until tender, turning serveral times, about 25 minutes. Brush with reserved marinade during final 10 minutes of cooking. Makes 3 to 4 servings.

Near Oxford

PICTOU COUNTY HODGE PODGE

This is a true harvest delight, a combination of garden-fresh vegetables at their peak of flavor.

4 to		1 to
6 cups	chopped fresh vegetables,*	1.5 L
1/4 lb	salt pork, cut in strips	125 g
1	medium onion, chopped	1
1 cup	light cream	250 mL
2 tbsp	butter	25 mL

In large saucepan, cook vegetables in boiling salted water just until tender. (Start with those requiring the longest cooking time and add others so all will be tender at the same time.) Drain vegetables, reserving 1/2 cup (125 mL) cooking liquid.

Meanwhile, in skillet, fry salt pork pieces until crisp (these are called scrunchions). Remove pork and add onion to fat in skillet; sauté until tender. Add reserved liquid, cream, butter and scrunchions. Bring just to boiling point and add to cooked vegetables. Serve piping hot. Makes 6 to 8 servings.

*Use any combination of fresh vegetables you like: small new potatoes, peas, baby carrots, green onions, string beans, broccoli or cauliflower florets.

'DOWN EAST' VEGGIE CHOWDER

3 tbsp	butter	50 mL
1/2 cup	chopped onion	125 mL
1 cup	chopped carrots	250 mL
1-1/2 cups	cubed potato	375 mL
1 tsp	salt	5 mL
1/4 tsp	each garlic powder, nutmeg & ground pepper	1 mL
2 tbsp	instant chicken bouillon powder	25 mL
1/2 cup	chopped broccoli or other green vegetable	125 mL
1 cup	water	250 mL
1 tbsp	cornstarch	15 mL
2 cups	milk	500 mL
2 tbsp	sour cream or yogurt (optional)	25 mL

In heavy saucepan, melt butter. Stir in onions, carrots, potato, seasonings and bouillon powder. Simmer covered for 10 minutes. Add broccoli and cook for 5 minutes longer. Transfer to blender. Add water and process until vegetables are coarsely chopped or to desired consistency. Return to saucepan. Mix cornstarch and milk; stir into vegetable mixture and cook for 2 minutes or until heated through. Add sour cream (if using). Makes 6 servings.

Halifax

Voglers Cove

BAKED STUFFED HADDOCK

This recipe is popular with South-Shore cooks and hungry guests.

3 to 4 lb	haddock	1.5 to 2 kg
2 cups	fresh breadcrumbs	500 mL
1 tsp	salt	5 mL
	Pepper and marjoram to taste	
1	small onion, minced	1
1/4 cup	melted butter	50 mL
1/4 cup	hot water	50 mL
4	bacon slices	4

Clean fish and let stand in salted ice water to firm flesh. Combine remaining ingredients except bacon. Dry inside of fish with paper towels. Stuff fish with breadcrumb mixture, set in baking dish and place bacon slices on top.

Bake in 450°F (230°C) oven for 10 to 12 minutes per inch (2.5 cm) thickness of fish, including stuffing, or until thickest part flakes easily with fork. Makes 6 servings.

Peggy's Cove

PLANKED SALMON MERSEY LODGE

Planking salmon is a time honoured method for preparing this delicious fish, originating with the local MicMac Indians. The hot plank cooks the skin side of the fish while the hot fire sears the surface locking in the juices. Today planked salmon is a special treat along the South Shore. It is enjoyed by hundreds of local people at the Annual Firemen's Supper in Greenfield. Over the years people from around the globe have been introduced to this special preparation while staying at Bowater Mersey's "Mersey Lodge". Guests are able to witness the preparation at each step as they enjoy the warmth of the huge fireplace and watch the sun set over the river. Chief Cook, Laurie DeMone, and his assistant, Arthur Anthony, are always willing to answer questions from the curious.
(Haddock, Halibut, Cod and Sea Bass may also be planked with excellent results).

10 lb	fresh salmon	22 kg
1 tsp	each seasoning salt and table salt	5 mL
1/2 tsp	white pepper	2 mL
1/4 cup	fresh lemon juice	50 mL
	Melted butter	

Clean and dress salmon. Fillet on both sides of back bone. Place salmon on tray — skin side down. With surgical tweezers remove all bones. Mix together seasoning salt, white pepper, and salt. Shake seasoning mixture over salmon. Pour lemon juice over salmon and marinate for 2 hours. Heat a clean hardwood plank placed upright in front of fireplace for about 15 minutes until it is hot. Place salmon on plank and secure with green maple twigs that have had their bark removed. Use small nails to nail the twigs to the plank. Place in front of fire (with a lot of hot coals) and cook until fish is golden brown and flaky. Depending on the size and heat of the fire, the fish will be about one or two (and perhaps three) feet from the fire. Use the back of your hand to check the "heat" of the fire. After about 20 to 25 minutes, the plank should be turned 180 degrees to allow the fish to be cooked more evenly. Cook for a further 20 to 25 minutes (less time will be needed for a grilse; more time for a large salmon), in this upside down position until flaky. Don't overcook as the heat of the plank will continue cooking the fish after it has been taken from the fire. Remove from plank and spread well with melted butter.

Cut salmon in 12 pieces and serve on a platter or individual dishes. Serve with scalloped potatoes, fresh buttered green peas, fresh broccoli with cheese sauce and a lemon wedge. Makes 12 servings.

Marys River

BANNOCK

Scottish lassies believed this bread enhanced their beauty and added sweetness to their disposition.

3 cups	all-purpose flour	750 mL
1 tbsp	granulated sugar	15 mL
2 tbsp	baking powder	25 mL
1 tsp	salt	5 mL
1/2 cup	light cream	125 mL
1-1/2 cups	milk	375 mL

Sift together dry ingredients three times. Add cream and milk and mix quickly; dough will be soft. Turn into greased 9 x 9 inch (23 x 23 cm) baking pan. Pat top with spoon dipped in milk, but do not smooth too much. Bake in 400°F (200°C) oven 25 to 30 minutes. Makes about 14 pieces.

Lunenburg

ROAST GOOSE WITH APRICOT APPLE STUFFING

1	goose (9 lb/about 4 kg)	1
1/2 cup	lemon juice	125 mL
	Salt and freshly ground pepper	
4 cups	boiling water	1 L
1/2 cup	red wine	125 mL
1 tbsp	molasses	15 mL

Remove all loose fat from goose. Wipe goose inside and out with damp cloth; dry thoroughly. Rub goose inside and out with lemon juice. Sprinkle cavity lightly with salt and pepper. Fill neck and body cavities with stuffing. Skewer or sew cavity closed and truss with string to secure legs, wings and neck skin to body. Using a needle or skewer, prick skin all over to allow fat to escape during roasting, being careful not to prick meat. Place goose breast side up on rack in shallow roasting pan.

In saucepan, combine water, wine and molasses; bring to boil. Pour half boiling liquid over goose. Roast uncovered in 400°F (200°C) oven for 30 minutes. Reduce heat to 325°F (160°C); Turn goose onto its side and roast for 1 hour. Pour off and discard liquid in pan. Turn goose onto other side; pour remaining hot liquid over goose; roast for 1 hour or until juices run clear when goose is pricked with skewer.

APRICOT APPLE STUFFING

1 cup	dried apricots	250 mL
3	tart apples, peeled and chopped	3
4 cups	fresh bread crumbs	1 L
1 tsp	salt	5 mL
1/2 tsp	each dried sage and thyme	2 mL
1/4 tsp	cinnamon	1 mL

In saucepan, cover apricots with water; bring to boil. Remove from heat; allow to stand 10 minutes; drain. Chop apricots. In large bowl, combine all ingredients. Mix thoroughly.

Menu

Smoked Salmon Pâté.
Toast Melba.

Roast Goose.
Pan Gravy.   Chestnut Stuffing.
Roast Potatoes. Red Cabbage.
Honey Glazed Carrots.

Fresh Pineapple Sherbert.

COTTAGE CHEESE MUFFINS

The Sunrise Trail stretches along the Northumberland coast to the Strait of Canso. The sandy beaches are a wonderful ocean playground and the Trail which forms part of the province's vital dairy belt is home to an excellent selection of dairy products including wholesome cottage cheese.

1/2 cup	butter	125 mL
2 cups	brown sugar	500 mL
	Grated peel of 1 lemon	
1	egg	1
2 cups	creamed cottage cheese	500 mL
2 cups	all-purpose flour	500 mL
1 tsp	salt	5 mL
1/2 tsp	baking soda	2 mL
1 cup	raisins	250 mL
1/4 cup	milk	50 mL

Cream butter and half the brown sugar until light. Add lemon peel and egg; beat well. Add remaining brown sugar and cottage cheese. Mix thoroughly.

Stir in flour, salt, soda, raisins and milk. Fill greased muffin tins 3/4 full. Bake in 350°F (180°C) oven for 30 minutes. Makes 24 muffins.

PUFFY PUMPKIN PANCAKES

1 cup	all-purpose flour	250 m
1 tbsp	granulated sugar	15 n
2 tsp	baking soda	10 n
1/2 tsp	salt	2 n
1/2 tsp	cinnamon	2 n
1 cup	milk	250 n
1/2 cup	cooked pumpkin purée (fresh or canned)	125 n
2	egg yolks, lightly beaten	
2 tbsp	melted butter	25 n
2	egg whites, stiffly beaten	

Sift together dry ingredients. Combine milk, pumpkin purée, e

...lks and butter. Add to dry ingredients; stir until evenly moisten-
...d. Fold in egg whites. For each pancake, pour 1/3 cup (75 mL) batter
...hot greased griddle; cook until golden on both sides. Serve with
...ot Cider Sauce (recipe follows). Makes 4 servings.

...ot Cider Sauce:

...4 cup	apple cider or juice	175 mL
...2 cup	brown sugar	125 mL
...2 cup	light corn syrup	125 mL
...tbsp	butter	25 mL
...2 tsp	lemon juice	2 mL
...nch	each of cinnamon and nutmeg	Pinch

...saucepan, combine all ingredients. Bring to boil, reduce heat and
...mmer, uncovered, 15 minutes. Makes 1-1/4 cups (300 mL).

PUMPKIN PIE

1-1/2 cups	canned or cooked pumpkin purée	375 mL
1-1/4 cups	whole milk	300 mL
3/4 cup	light cream	175 mL
3/4 cup	brown sugar	175 mL
1 tsp	cinnamon	5 mL
1/2 tsp	ginger	2 mL
1/4 tsp	nutmeg	1 mL
1/2 tsp	salt	2 mL
3	eggs	3
2	unbaked pie shells (9 in/23 cm)	2
	Whipped cream	

In top of double boiler over hot water, mix together pumpkin, milk
and cream. Cover and heat just to boiling.

Meanwhile, in mixing bowl, combine brown sugar, spices and
salt. Stir in eggs. Gradually stir in pumpkin mixture. Pour into pie
shells.

Bake in 425°F (220°C) oven for 10 minutes, then reduce heat to
350°F (180°C) and bake for 45 minutes longer or until knife inserted in centre comes out clean. Chill. Serve with whipped cream.

Louisburg

RABBIT PIE

The popularity of rabbit pie is testimony to the French heritage in Cape Breton. Today, it is usually served on Christmas Eve.

1	rabbit (about 3 lb/1.5 kg), cut in pieces	1
1 tbsp	vinegar	15 mL
	Salt	
	All-purpose flour	
2 tbsp	shortening	25 mL
1 cup	minced onion	250 mL
1 cup	minced celery	250 mL
	Pepper, mace	
	Biscuit dough*	

Place rabbit pieces in large saucepan or soup kettle. Cover with water; add vinegar and a little salt. Boil gently, partially covered, until tender. Drain, reserving stock.

Dredge rabbit pieces with flour. In Dutch oven, melt shortening; add onion, celery and rabbit pieces. Cook, stirring often, until rabbit is browned on all sides. Remove meat from bones and cut it into bite-sized pieces. Place in well-greased baking dish. Cover with reserved stock; season with a little salt, pepper and mace. Cover with biscuit dough. Bake in 450°F (230°C) oven 20 to 25 minutes or until top is golden brown. Makes 4 to 6 servings.

Ingonish

*One double pie pastry may be substituted for biscuit dough. Line a 10-inch (25 cm) pie plate with pastry. Prepare filling as above. Top with lattice strips of pastry. Bake in 450°F (230°C) oven 10 minutes; reduce heat to 350°F (180°C) and bake 20 minutes longer.

CAPE BRETON OATCAKES

Try this traditional Nova Scotia favorite with tea or buttermilk.

3 cups	rolled oats	750 mL
3 cups	all-purpose flour	750 mL
1 cup	granulated sugar	250 mL
1/2 tsp	salt	2 mL
2 cups	shortening	500 mL
1/4 cup	cold water	50 mL

Combine dry ingredients. Work in shortening with fingers; stir in water. Place in greased 18 x 12 inch (45 x 30 cm) jelly-roll pan or on baking sheet. Spread mixture over pan and into corners. With rolling pin, flatten mixture until smooth and firm. With greased knife, cut into 2-inch (5 cm) squares. Bake in 350°F (180°C) oven about 15 minutes or until lightly browned. Serve plain or with butter. Makes 60 squares.

Louisburg

Louisburg